Mark Blaeuer

Surfacing Below

SurVision Books

First published in 2025 by
SurVision Books
Dublin, Ireland
Reggio di Calabria, Italy
www.survisionmagazine.com

Copyright © Mark Blaeuer, 2025

Cover image by M-Art Production

Design © SurVision Books, 2025

ISBN: 978-1-912963-58-4

This book is in copyright. No part of this publication may be reproduced, stored in a retrieval system, or transmitted in any form or by any means without the prior permission in writing from the publisher.

Acknowledgments

Grateful acknowledgment is made to the editors of the following, in which some of these poems, or versions of them, originally appeared:

Bone Orchard Poetry: "Indulgences" and "What Once Was Darkness"

The Camel Saloon: "Religion at First Sight" and "Surfacing Below" (as "Allegory")

The Dead Mule School of Southern Literature: "Prospector"

Ink Sweat and Tears: "Harlan & Siv"

Otoliths: "An Afterworld Northwest of Hudson Bay" and "Theology"

SurVision Magazine: "A Gala to Remember," "After the Shuttles," "At the Grave of John Swingendorf," "By Heart," "Current Weather," "Desert Story," "Don't Look, Never Look," "Farewell to Balance," "Hyperrealism," "Innerborough," "Miracle," "Old School," "Perfection" (as "Perfection Everywhere"), "To the Radiant," and "Vitrine"

Uut Poetry: "Reality Show" (as "Here, Nowhere, There, and Everywhere at Once")

CONTENTS

Innerborough	5
Farewell to Balance	6
Don't Look, Never Look	8
By Heart	9
Current Weather	10
To the Radiant	11
Old School	12
Indulgences	13
A Gala to Remember	14
An Afterworld Northwest of Hudson Bay	15
Desert Story	16
Prospector	17
Perfection	18
Religion at First Sight	19
Hyperrealism	20
What Once Was Darkness	21
Reality Show	22
Harlan & Siv	23
At the Grave of John Swingendorf	24
Theology	25
After the Shuttles	26
Surfacing Below	27
Miracle	28
Vitrine	29

Innerborough

Daily I ran down Upper Street and turned
at the mansion, on my way to buy darkness
from a 7-Eleven. Some days, empty-handed, I'd
saber-charge over broken sidewalk, a lad of empire.
One Sabbath, edging past the ghost daughters'
bicycles balanced on pedestals, and the open window

to the bedroom of the matriarch always in
a coma, I scrutinized the row of black-painted
iron palings. Behind, in the yard's northeast corner,
lay a tarnished bronze plaque half-buried at ground level,
shaded by ancient butternut trees. I stretched an arm
through to whisk off rotting leaves, dirt—the tabula rasa layer—

and finally struck words. Cast by the DAR
perhaps a century before, the text hove into focus:
Here we commemorate a place where
you realized the first battle of the War of 1812
occurred in 2181, on Indian Ocean floor. This only
deepened that house's mystery for me.

Farewell to Balance

We were having a nice
day until four Nazis appeared.
Not neo-Nazis but historic Germans,
who blitzed the conversation in our breakfast nook.
An SS officer, wearing an eyepatch
and fresh from South America, insisted
I brew coffee. He chose a medium blend
more virulent than I knew
was in the larder—from Brazil or Peru,
I don't remember which. When the Nazis finally
left, I examined his cup; despite
the fuss he made, he hadn't drunk much.
The now-cold liquid was thin,
transparent, with extremely coarse sediments.
At first I thought the pebble-sized grains
might have been peanuts he'd dropped
into his beverage, for the hell of it,
but I soon realized the objects were
snails—still moving.

Ah, the worst part.
Instead of sealing the cup and its contents
in a hazardous waste enclosure—
how would I have known to do that?—
I spilled some on the floor, whereupon
a wicker den set sprang up, buckling our bas-relief tile.
When the furniture was taken away,
a bedroom suite replaced it: Mom's, it was called,
I discovered later. When that was hauled off,

a third phase: Dad's workbench.
We phoned the Center for Disease Control, whose
experts arrived. They said wicker
is a nuisance to clean, but the parental
pieces could obviously reproduce. Lying on the bed
or brushing past the bench
releases spores onto your clothing, spores
you might then unwittingly transfer
to countless other locations.

And there is no cure, except
annihilation of all life on the planet.

Don't Look, Never Look

Again, the xanthic curvature
retirees seek through
glass.

A vagabond housed at
memory's igloo
drops in

for a pint, thus giddily remembered
some planned opus—
Weltmeister

accordion version of 1938's *Encyclopedia Britannica*—
riches unto corporate had
spark

flared up madder like hills. Instead,
this interrogative
sunlight

hobbles toward the answer
idling in a mink
apron.

By Heart

Long appointed, village elders enter a charnel house
reserved for birth. They stand silent over a woman, then—
after severing umbilical—hand her the wet
razor. From memory she incises circles, one, another,
on a newborn's face. The elders rub bitumen
into cuts, as she fondles her necklace. Soon
she'll knit a pouch to hold the ritual blade (her child to prosper).

A score of years later, the woman's daughter gives pure life
to William Blake and twelve extras, mostly
angels. Blake, born an elder, furrows his left brain at cherubim
writing a dirge. Ugly, profound, their unvoiced lyrics
etch a halo in the face of courage.

Current Weather

We scientifically surveyed 100 subjects
in a soundproof, windowless room:
34 said it was raining outside; 21 believed it
to be snowing; 18 were adamant
it was clear, the temperature 5 below zero;
14 responded that it was cloudy but well
over 90 degrees; 8 admitted to being unsure
of anything; 3 yelled, *Death to canvassers!*
2 volunteered to go check actual conditions,
if they could find the door.

A brawl warning remains in effect.

To the Radiant

You assume an ocean
of coloring books, e.g. Gauguin,
to be fodder-in-typhoon.
Of a dawn you fill, matching solar pace,
tipsy on a 48-pack.
With rain to patter a low noon,
you redden outriggers in the mind.
Heavy dusk: a Cuttle Ink crayon exceeds all
accidental myth, osmosing toward
the blue—no, bluest—lorikeet.
Under a mango-pulp moon
you tear out pages, scissoring
wildly to fold,
to glue,
manila journey upward to palm fronds,
a tropic nest
in which to close your eyes.

Old School

A self-important ship,
its four-letter unword thrusting
aside Johnny Bucco,
rolled around our scene
in girth, in tonnage,
amid the flotsam.
Young was I, filtering
Captain Ahab's Omnibus
for newsy plankton.
Juvenile feeder in the Zygote Sea
was I, as saltettes raised and lowered
fragile world, our double-hung
sash tall as a foremast,
with their chained harpoon.
The lesson: gel coat laminate
interpretive panel, high tensile
mount.

Indulgences

Vendors on Xanadu subway
hawk their effigy food,
plasticware and paper napkins
next to a ticket booth.

A balladeer by a staircase
sings out the wrongs of our planet.
She holds an object carved of polished wood,
open at both ends, hollow as a drum:

a woman's torso.
Punctuating lament, she
hits her eerie cylinder with a stick.
We all walk home, hungry.

A Gala to Remember

Art-gangs advertised a rumble,
a plein air fray. Out-of-towners flocked
at superbly green lawn, only to be
snuffed when they ignored the adage
that you don't bring an easel to a gunfight.
Even the Homeowner Association fell powerless,
which was okay because John Constable
materialized. Seeped out from his tomb
of nearly two centuries, he meant vengeance.
His post-mortem fame as vigilante
sprang from having grown twelve feet tall
while a specter in Hampstead. Now he
infused life in the broken limbs
of those slain, and restored the innocent,
who ambled off to thank their host
for a lovely time.

An Afterworld Northwest of Hudson Bay

> —text found in Asen Balikci, "Netsilik" (page 426),
> *Handbook of North American Indians,* Vol. 5

The energetic
hunters and tattooed women
live in eternal
bliss
in villages located high
in the sky
or very deep
under the tundra.

The lazy hunters remain just
below the crust
of the earth;
they are perpetually hungry
and apathetic, and
their only food
is
the butterfly.

Desert Story

The first jet arrows north.
A phantom intercepts it, chasing south. They sweep
low in the moonlight, dodging saguaro. They trade fire high
over the ruins of Phoenix, soaring. The spirit
presses, launches one sidewinder missile—

forcing the young Navajo pilot to land.
His grounded plane's fuselage
vibrates from nose to an exhaust-hole at its tail.
Out the cockpit climbs a tribal elder,
face terraced like a strip mine.

Prospector

I trace the Rockies
to a southern lair.
Above, snowy crags. I stop
at a cabin, knock.
Some bearded geezer
pokes his head out, snarls, "Whaddaya want?"
I feel I've struck Texas.
He spits. "Them *ain't* the Rockies,
and this *ain't* Texas."
I ask, "Which mountains are they?"
He squints up at the peaks,
then back at me.
"Hell, ain't no mountains around here."
Adjacent, a guy is plowing hillside
with mules.
His beat-up '64 Impala wagon is parked
on a dirt driveway leading down to the main road.
I slide in and
rev,
amazed not that it's unlocked, keys in ignition,
but that it works.
In rearview I glimpse the owner
scowling.

Perfection

The omelet wore Velcro pajamas
after it won an award for selling a broken toy
in Great Dismal Swamp.

Venus bilked swordfish at the colosseum
until her epic slime
lionized some antiquated penguin.

And me?
Well, as Dr. Brinkley told one of his goat glands,
"Wipe that face off your smile."

Religion at First Sight

Our catcher lofts a magic souvenir
down the right field line. Stinging my
hands, his globe fashioned of antique horsehide
with (miniscule in sweet spot, India ink)
an eephus entitled "Rube"—*To live in such a place
is something. To work every day at something
is something more, and to love baseball is something
else.* High-driven sphere upon our sanctified
bleachers.

Hyperrealism

Fire morphs into a Renaissance
warehouse, then speciating hadrosaurs,
planetesimals, and the actual
Big Bang. *Typical,* says an expert
on debutante coteries.

Politicians fly
yachts over a battery of windmills
aimed at Amsterdam, ermine
turbines on the right flank. *Exquisite,* says an aesthete
under a sombrero.

Night takes evening by one arm, propels
light across the ring to sag
at a turnbuckle. Raucous gnostics jeer
in the Milky Way's musty Entropic Room. *Fall,*
says our bogus referee.

What Once Was Darkness

Winter dawns,
radioactive blood,
rare choice in the palette
of Erebus
imbued with bioluminescent
glow.

Reality Show

I rise in support of House Bill 27 Degrees Kelvin.
A millstone dangles off one ear of Alien Economics,
opera shucked and blaring out the selfsame ear.
I want you to grok that what appears to be a Mig-19
is really a spice cake, even though Gettysburg

shred our most hallowed jujube.
So said Thomas the Rhymer. I can't say another word. This
Queen Anne lincolnlogged in his six hands
impresseth, unless it doesn't, in which outlandish case
reap poisonous bamboo.

She clinks a few calliopes together. She nukes a venison
soufflé. She spanks Ecuador. The essence of quietus
onto her gaudily parachutes, as panoramic had
them Busby Berkeley Bipeds. Or munchkin deodorant salvos
intervene.

Harlan & Siv

Euglena Harlan presides at our
Church of Gullibility in the Vale,
arraigned for murder of his younger self,
prosecutor Marat Siv marshalling
arguments, exhibits, testimony
against the Judge-Who-Rules-at-Pulpit.

During a recess, Siv confronts Harlan
at the rear of the sanctuary, with these words:
"I have a nose for justice!" Said schnoz
leaps out of Siv's three-piece, hovers
noisily, then surges forward, impelling
Harlan swiftly up one aisle to a point

high above the altar (by sleight of snout).
Siv tolls, "Guilty! Guilty! Guilty!"
Harlan: "Get. Me. Down."
Siv frees him, "You're a good sport,
Your Honor." And slips that precious proboscis
into his vest pocket for next time.

At the Grave of John Swingendorf

In a predestined flower
bed, I kneel to pick up a dirt clod that turns
out to be a concretion of coins, none larger than a quarter,
my luck changed. I pull the cluster apart, the coins pristine
with their little numismatic stands at base, the latest from 1967.
Some of the coins turn out to be magazines, from 1958, '56, '54 . . .
One of the magazines turns out to be an alligator gar,
      eight and a half feet long
and taxidermied, ready for wall-mounting. Swingendorf
was an ichthyologist, I deduce. Not to mention a film buff,
judging by 35 mm footage in the clump. He also was
      slim, with Brylcreemed
hair, a suit (narrow tie as bisector), and horn-rim glasses,
per dead reckoning. John,
you were John

and/or a telegram of platinum.

Theology

Caged, it preens feathers,
wingspan larger than
created realm,
each human a steel bar
rendering instinct useless.

The ancient retains neither
signet of self
nor any urge to feel
equations wriggling in its beak,
as happened eons ago.

Improbably,
it hides among numbers now.

After the Shuttles

A Saturn rocket stands at attention,
set to blast my dusty, dented truck into space.

We assemble atop a gantry, the pickup like a cherry on a sundae—
but the tires are flat.

The astronauts all snicker inside their helmets, and one says,
"There went your prize for being American."

Surfacing Below

I grab my first aid kit.
The target house near, I decide
to run there. Soon I'm on the highway,
stuck behind a marathon
of centenarians, most crawling.
I yell, "Hurry up, you old
people!" They reach a place where
they're supposed to rappel up a cliff,
and this slows them further, dogged
seniors moving two inches
every thousand years, covering
the precipice I have to ascend.
Unlatching my kit, I pull out
the bullwhip. CRACK! "Climb, suckers!
Hurry *up,* you *old* people!"
CRACK! "I'm responding to
a medical emergency!" Elders fall.
"Come on, damn it!" CRACK! Finally,
enough of the face clear, I
can elbow past, dropping a few
more. At top I dash to my
destination, family
at the door. "You're too late,"
they accuse, "He died." "Well, heck,"
I say, rummaging my kit
to find a baggie. "I was going
to administer this to your father: who
wants a doughnut hole?"

Miracle

A woman in her seventies gave birth, scarlet birth,
the baby twice-sired. One father,
a you-bet-your-life unorthodox rabbi, sported a military
cap and puffed on a Cuban cigar.
The second was a rather supple wax figure of a jitterbugging
    Chairman Mao.

Our scientists, laboring with calloused minds,
endeavor to understand how it happened.
Our televangelists portentously spew.
The woman's husband, Rhett Butler? Frankly,
his world ended before he was imagined.

Vitrine

Once, à la Brothers Grimm, a woman dwelt in a glass coffin.
She required neither food nor oxygen, yet she was alive
and, during business hours, awake. Her cozy home merited pride
    of place
near the cash register. She appeared comfortable, head atop a lace-
white cushion, the rest of her body gowned in cerise.
She was married to the famous journalist, Señor San Antonio y Oro
    de Madrid,
who was reportedly content to pursue his career without her,
and she seemed happy to carry on in his absence.
In no way did she consider herself deprived.

She was renowned for her excellent wit and fine laugh.
I chatted with her and enjoyed the privilege immensely. Turning
away for a moment, though, to record her comments
    in my notebook, I was startled
by a crash. Her coffin had fallen off its catafalque, shards everywhere.
    Three or four men—
perhaps employees of the store, perhaps her servants—
    ran to see about her and sweep up.
I, too, attempted to check on her condition and render assistance,
but one of the men announced, as if to spare me anguish
    or inconvenience,
that she was dead but luckily not disfigured.
On impulse I bought a plastic doll modeled after her—also, of course,
    available in the shop.

The item was not shrink wrapped, a process which might have evoked
the substance of her coffin. Rather, said femuncula portrayed
the lady as a black-robed adolescent. This thing was undoubtedly
 meant for children,
to be hung in a prominent location at Halloween, so as an adult
 I confess it frightened me.
I left these premises. The sky, what little I could detect among
 downtown buildings,
was overcast. As people walked by, I shook the doll in their faces
(most of the passersby reacted negatively) until my zeal abated.
I then sat upon an iron bench, alone
and clearing.

Selected Poetry Titles Published by SurVision Books

Contemporary Tangential Surrealist Poetry: An Anthology
Edited by Tony Kitt
ISBN 978-1-912963-44-7

Invasion: An Anthology of Ukrainian Poetry about the War
Edited by Tony Kitt
ISBN 978-1-912963-32-4

Noelle Kocot. *Humanity*
(New Poetics: USA)
ISBN 978-1-9995903-0-7

Marc Vincenz. *Einstein Fledermaus*
(New Poetics: USA)
ISBN 978-1-912963-20-1

Helen Ivory. *Maps of the Abandoned City*
(New Poetics: England)
ISBN 978-1-912963-04-1

Tony Kitt. *The Magic Phlute*
(New Poetics: Ireland)
ISBN 978-1-912963-08-9

Clayre Benzadón. *Liminal Zenith*
(New Poetics: USA)
ISBN 978-1-912963-11-9

Thomas Townsley. *Tangent of Ardency*
(New Poetics: USA)
ISBN 978-1-912963-15-7

Mikko Harvey & Jake Bauer. *Idaho Falls*
(Winner of James Tate Poetry Prize 2018)
ISBN 978-1-912963-02-7

John Bradley. *Spontaneous Mummification*
(Winner of James Tate Poetry Prize 2019)
ISBN 978-1-912963-13-3

Charles Kell. *Pierre Mask*
(Winner of James Tate Poetry Prize 2019)
ISBN 978-1-912963-19-5

Charles Borkhuis. *Spontaneous Combustion*
(Winner of James Tate Poetry Prize 2021)
ISBN 978-1-912963-30-0

Noah Falck and Matt McBride. *Prerecorded Weather*
(Winner of James Tate Poetry Prize 2022)
ISBN 978-1-912963-39-3

Jeffrey Cyphers Wright. *Fuel for Love*
(Winner of James Tate Poetry Prize 2023)
ISBN 978-1-912963-45-4

George Kalamaras. *That Moment of Wept*
ISBN 978-1-9995903-7-6

George Kalamaras. *Through the Silk-Heavy Rains*
ISBN 978-1-912963-28-7

Guillaume Apollinaire. *Ocean of Earth: Selected Poems*
Translated from French by Matthew Geden
ISBN 978-1-912963-40-9

Order our books from survisionmagazine.com

www.ingramcontent.com/pod-product-compliance
Lightning Source LLC
Chambersburg PA
CBHW061315040426
42444CB00010B/2653